Get your Grammar in order with CGP!

If you're after unbeatable SATs Grammar prep, look no further!
This SAT Buster is the best way to make sure pupils are totally ready.

It's full of questions covering every Grammar topic in the SATs
— plus mixed practice pages to see how much they've learnt.

There are even friendly self-assessment boxes throughout the book
and a handy scoresheet to check their progress overall.

What CGP is all about

Our sole aim here at CGP is to produce the highest quality books
— carefully written, immaculately presented and
dangerously close to being funny.

Then we work our socks off to get them out to you
— at the cheapest possible prices.

Published by CGP

Editors: Tom Carney, Rachel Craig-McFeely, Melissa Gardner, Heather Gregson, Kelsey Hammond, Catherine Heygate

ISBN: 978 1 78294 275 7

Printed by Elanders Ltd, Newcastle upon Tyne.
Clipart from Corel®

Based on the classic CGP style created by Richard Parsons.

Text, design, layout and original illustrations © Coordination Group Publications Ltd. (CGP) 2019
All rights reserved.

Photocopying this book is not permitted, even if you have a CLA licence.
Extra copies are available from CGP with next day delivery. • 0800 1712 712 • www.cgpbooks.co.uk

Contents

Section 1 – Types of Word

Nouns 2
Singular and plural nouns 3
Types of noun 4
Pronouns 6
Determiners 8
Verbs 9
Adjectives 12
Adverbs 14
Mixed practice 16

Section 2 – Clauses, Phrases and Sentences

Sentences 20
Paragraphs 21
Phrases 22
Clauses 24
Relative clauses 26
Mixed practice 28

Section 3 – Conjunctions and Prepositions

Co-ordinating conjunctions 32
Subordinating conjunctions 33
Prepositions 34
Mixed practice 36

Section 4 – Sentence Structure and Tense

Subject and object 38
Active and passive voice 39
Past, present and future tenses 40
Verbs with 'have' 42
Verbs with '-ing' 43
Mixed practice 44

Section 5 – Writing Style

Standard vs. Non-Standard 46
Formal and informal writing 48
Mixed practice 49

Section 6 – Making and Choosing Words

Word families 51
Prefixes 52
Suffixes 54
Making verbs 56
Synonyms 58
Antonyms 59
Mixed practice 60

Glossary 62
Scoresheet 64

Here's what you have to do...

In Year 6 you have to take some tests called the SATs.
This book will help you do well in the grammar bit of the tests.

 This is a Grammagator — it can handle even the trickiest grammar questions.

Your aim is to become a Grammagator.

Work through the questions in the book. When you finish a topic, add up your marks and write them in the scoresheet at the end of the book.

Then, put a tick in the box at the end of the topic to show how you got on.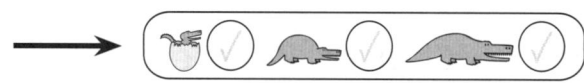

 If you got a lot of grammar questions wrong, put a tick in the circle on the left. Don't worry — every Grammagator has to start somewhere. Make sure you know your grammar rules inside out, then have another go.

If you're happy with some grammar questions but still got a few wrong, put a tick in the middle circle. Ask your teacher to help you work out the areas you need more practice on.

 If you felt really confident and got nearly all the grammar right, tick the circle on the right.

Congratulations — you're a Grammagator!

Grammar Hints and Tips

Even the best Grammagators find grammar tricky sometimes, but don't worry — this page will give you some handy advice for getting to grips with good grammar.

1. **Learn** the **main parts** of speech.

    The <u>mouse</u> <u>nibbled</u> the <u>juicy</u> raisin.

    Noun
    (a naming word)

    Verb
    (a doing or being word)

    Adjective
    (a describing word)

2. Make sure you can **identify** the different **parts** of a **sentence**.

    <u>The cat sprinted across the kitchen</u> <u>when it saw the mouse</u>.

    Main Clause
    (the most important clause)

    Subordinate Clause
    (the less important clause)

3. Make sure that the **verb agrees** with whoever is doing the action.

    The <u>cat licks</u> its lips.   The <u>cats lick</u> their lips.

    There is **only one** cat, so the verb needs to be **singular**.

    There's **more than one** cat, so the verb needs to be **plural**.

4. Check that **verbs** are written correctly in each **tense**.

    It <u>has eaten</u> the mouse.   It <u>ate</u> the mouse.

    Not It <u>has ate</u> the mouse.   **Not** It <u>eaten</u> the mouse.

5. Know how to spot **Non-Standard English**, like double negatives.

    It has <u>not</u> eaten <u>no</u> mouse.   It has not eaten the mouse.

    This is a **double negative**.   This is **Standard English**.

Section 1 — Types of Word

Nouns

Nouns are the words we use to name things — people, places, custard...
Work through these questions to make sure you can spot them a mile off.

1) Tick the words below which are nouns.

   jam ☐   softly ☐   massive ☐   actor ☐   assembly ☐

   hat ☐   happy ☐   Hannah ☐   confident ☐   headache ☐

   Choose one of the nouns from above, and use it in a sentence.

   ....

   2 marks

2) Underline all the nouns. Then write another noun to replace each noun. *Make sure the nouns you choose make sense.*

   <u>Fran</u> carried the <u>flowers</u> carefully.   Nathan   jelly

   The dentist checked my teeth.   ....

   There's a new house in our road.   ....

   We found a worm under the soil.   ....

   There are lots of fish in the sea.   ....

   2 marks

3) Add your own nouns to the passage below.

   Sam waited for everyone to leave the ...., then opened her rucksack. Inside, there was a ...., a .... and a .... She was pleased she'd remembered everything. She waited by the .... for her friend, ..., to arrive.

   2 marks

Nouns are the first step on the journey to becoming a Grammagator. How did you do? Tick the box.

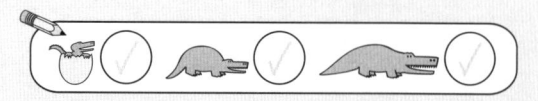

Singular and plural nouns

Nouns can be singular or plural depending on whether there's one or many of something.

1) Circle the plural nouns below.

   magnet   jumper   lizards   wishes

   gardens   festival   babies   actress

   'Plural' means more than one.

   2 marks

2) Cross out the incorrect form of the noun in each sentence.

   My (**picture / pictures**) has lots of fields in the (**background / backgrounds**).

   Our class (**robot / robots**) has (**arm / arms**) made of cardboard (**tube / tubes**).

   The teacher gave each (**child / children**) a (**bag / bags**) of (**sweet / sweets**).

   2 marks

3) The plural nouns in **bold** are incorrect. Write the correct versions on the lines.

   one cherry, two **cherrys** ....   one torch, two **torchs** ....

   one man, two **mans** ....   one fairy, two **fairys** ....

   one fox, two **foxs** ....   one half, two **halfs** ....

   2 marks

4) Rewrite each sentence below, changing the nouns in **bold** into plurals.

   Dad found the **cat** hiding under the **bush**.

   ....

   The **thief** stole the **ruby** from the **cabinet**.

   ....

   2 marks

*Grammagators aren't foxed by tricky plural nouns.
Are you? Tick the box to show how well you did.*

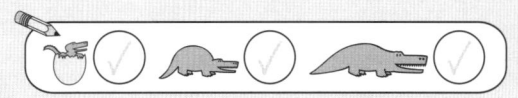

Types of noun

There are several different types of noun to tackle on these pages — you're welcome...

1) Use the words in the box to complete the definitions.

| ideas | general | proper | groups |

Common nouns are .... words for things, animals and people.

The names of specific people, places or things are .... nouns.

Collective nouns are words for .... of animals or people.

Abstract nouns are words for .... and concepts.

2 marks

2) In the boxes below, write whether each noun is common (C) or proper (P).

station ☐   Greece ☐   rhino ☐   Jason ☐   biscuits ☐

waiter ☐   school ☐   April ☐   carrot ☐   tornado ☐

2 marks

3) Sort the words below into the correct columns.

sandwich	swarm	~~bravery~~	horde
fear	Liverpool	hamster	arena
Friday	patience	flock	Stefan

Common Nouns	Proper Nouns	Collective Nouns	Abstract Nouns
....	....	....	......bravery......
....	....	....	....
....	....	....	....

2 marks

Section 1 — Types of Word

Types of noun

4) Rewrite this sentence, replacing the words in **bold** with proper nouns.

   The girl took **her dog** for a walk.

   ....

   2 marks

5) Match each collective noun to the correct animal.

   | gaggle | pack | army | herd | shoal |

   | geese | cows | dogs | fish | ants |

   (gaggle — geese)

   2 marks

6) Circle all the abstract nouns in the passage below. There are four in total.

   An abstract noun is a name for something that you cannot see, hear, smell or touch.

   We are all very impressed with the dedication of the Year Six students this year. They have taken on a lot of responsibility for their work and acted with kindness towards younger pupils. We will miss their enthusiasm next year.

   2 marks

7) Write two different sentences that use all three of the nouns provided:

   London   **taxi**   **gorilla**

   ....

   Mr Lewis   **books**   **classroom**

   ....

   2 marks

Grammagators are no common bunch — they know nouns like a mouse knows cheese. Are you one of them?

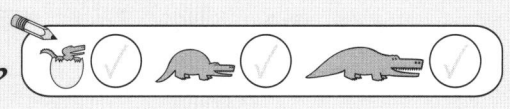

Pronouns

Pronouns are words that can replace nouns. They help your writing flow better.

1) Circle the pronouns in each of the sentences below. *There may be more than one pronoun in a sentence.*

   We have a rabbit.   He lives by himself.   Kai and I are friends.

   Ben stopped them.   Mum helped me.   Did you make it yourself?

   2 marks

2) Write down who or what the underlined pronouns refer to in these sentences.

   Rinah and Mohammed missed Ian's party because <u>they</u> were on holiday.

   ....

   A few pets, like dogs and cats, eat meat. <u>Some</u>, like rabbits, prefer vegetables.

   ....

   2 marks

3) Replace the underlined phrases with the correct pronoun.

   Jo and I baked a cake, and then <u>Jo and I</u> ate <u>the cake</u>.

   When pieces of writing have cohesion, it is clear how their words and sentences fit together. Pronouns help give your writing cohesion.

   Harry needs his running shoes, but <u>Harry</u> can't find <u>his running shoes</u>.

   Sven asked his parents for a new bike, but <u>Sven's parents</u> said no.

   My sister built a snowman, and then <u>my sister</u> knocked <u>the snowman</u> down.

   2 marks

Pronouns

4) Cross out the incorrect pronoun in the sentences below.

Gran says (**we** / **us**) can plant some vegetables, and she will help (**us** / **her**).

(**I** / **Me**) went on holiday, and my parents came with (**us** / **me**).

His teacher told (**he** / **him**) off because (**he** / **they**) was late for school.

(**Her** / **You**) should go to the shops and buy a present for (**they** / **them**).

2 marks

5) Circle all the **possessive pronouns** in the box below.

Possessive pronouns show who things belong to.

you   they   his   we   theirs   I   ours   it   hers   she   mine   he

2 marks

6) Draw lines to match each sentence with the correct possessive pronoun.

The car belongs to Steve and Alice.	It is mine.
We own the farm.	It is hers.
That's my model aeroplane.	It is theirs.
It's Sara's library book.	It is ours.

2 marks

Pronouns may be small, but they're important words for any budding Grammagator. Have you got them sorted?

Determiners

A determiner is a little word like 'a', 'the' or 'much' that goes before a noun or noun phrase. The articles 'a', 'an' and 'the' are the most common determiners, but there are lots more.

1) Rewrite each sentence using the correct determiner in brackets.

   The tunnel makes (**an** / **a**) echo when you talk.

   ....

   Do you have (**much** / **many**) money?

   ....

   It took (**one** / **three**) weeks to find a replacement for (**the** / **an**) dancing horse.

   ....

   2 marks

2) Put a tick in the boxes to show where determiners are needed in this passage.

   To play 'Blind Man's Bluff' you need ☐ blindfold. Secure it around ☐ player's head.

   Then everyone else hides in ☐ room and the blindfolded player looks for them.

   2 marks

3) Each of these sentences uses one determiner incorrectly.
   Circle the error, then write the correction on the dotted line.

   'an' only goes before vowel sounds. 'k' is a consonant so this should be 'a'.

   They have taught the monkey how to use (an) knife and fork. ......a......

   I've had the awful journey, so a hot bath is just what I need. ....

   Susie made much cakes for the baking competition. ....

   2 marks

Grammagators eat determiners for breakfast. Did you manage them all? Tick a box to show how you got on.

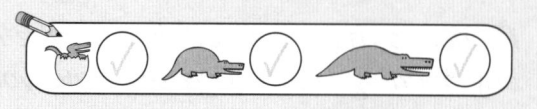

Section 1 — Types of Word   © CGP — not to be photocopied

Verbs

Verbs are doing or being words. You need to make sure that the verb agrees with the subject.

1) Underline the verbs in these sentences.

   Naughty koala bears make a terrible mess when they eat eucalyptus leaves.

   The hungry goat ate my favourite T-shirt and drank all the milk from the fridge.

   2 marks

2) Fill in the blanks with verbs from the box below.

   | **pitch** | **headed** | **arrived** | **cooked** |

   It was nearly dark when we .... at the campsite. I helped

   my brothers to .... the tent, then .... everyone

   some food. I was so tired that I .... to bed straight after that.

   2 marks

3) Tick the version of each sentence which uses verbs correctly.

   I entertain my friends. ☐   I entertains my friends. ☐

   Xavier look on top of the world. ☐   Xavier looks on top of the world. ☐

   2 marks

4) Read this sentence: **Adin discovers some old sardines under his bed.**

   What is the verb in this sentence?   ....

   1 mark

5) Match each subject in the grey boxes to the correct form of the verb.

   | it | | Mum and I | | she | | the children | | Mr Jones |

   | do | | does |

   2 marks

Section 1 — Types of Word

Verbs

6) Complete each sentence using the present tense form of the verb in brackets.

   My brother always ......refuses...... (to refuse) to go to bed on time.

   At school, we .... (to learn) to multiply numbers in our head.

   A chameleon .... (to change) colour to match its environment.

   The pirates .... (to guard) the treasure day and night.

   The shopkeeper .... (to be) now a suspect in the robbery.

   2 marks

7) Rewrite each sentence, changing the verbs so that they are written from a different point of view.

   My uncle flies to France, skis and learns French.

   They fly to France, ski and learn French.

   I visit relatives, eat and sing at Christmas.

   Peter

   Jared is very active, and swims or cycles every day.

   We

   2 marks

8) Write a sentence using the verbs given below.

   Remember to put the verbs in the correct form.

   to want   **to buy**

   ....

   to search   **to find**

   ....

   2 marks

Verbs

9) Underline the modal verbs in these sentences.

   Louis will lend us his van when we move house.

   Your sister said she would take us to the school play.

   Modal verbs are words like 'may' and 'shall' which often show how likely something is.

   They might move to Antarctica to study penguins.

   Anya's novel is really good — she ought to publish it.

   2 marks

10) In the boxes below, write whether the modal verb in each sentence shows **certainty** (C) or **possibility** (P).

    She might come with us. ☐   They will meet us there. ☐

    You shall mow the lawn. ☐   We may leave early. ☐

    2 marks

11) Rewrite these sentences using the correct verb from the brackets.

    When I was six, I (**can / will / could**) not reach this shelf.

    ....

    Pamina (**might / shall / will**) be right about that, but I'm not sure.

    ....

    2 marks

12) Tick the sentences which contain a modal verb.

    Siân would like to visit her uncle in Spain. ☐

    You ought to share that piece of cake with your brother. ☐

    After a long journey, the astronaut finally landed on the moon. ☐

    2 marks

Grammagators think verbs are nearly as tasty as pickled onions. How confident are you about verbs?

Adjectives

Adjectives are words that tell you more about a noun, e.g. Grammagators are <u>gigantic</u>.

1) Circle the adjective in each of the sentences below.

   This ice cream is delicious.   The heavy bags suddenly burst open.

   A bitter wind gripped the town.   My sister can be annoying sometimes.

   Surprisingly, Jin found a rare fossil. Dad bravely rode the largest horse.

   The swings in the park are broken.   Emma needed a strong coffee.

   2 marks

2) Choose an adjective to describe each noun below.

alligator ➡	picture ➡ ....
trousers ➡	factory ➡ ....
attic ➡	snail ➡ ....
village ➡	puppet ➡ ....
juice ➡	forest ➡ ....

   2 marks

3) Underline the adjectives in each sentence.
   Then choose another suitable adjective to replace each one.

   My cat, Tibbles, is <u>lively</u> and <u>friendly</u>.   ......slow......   ......lazy......

   A loud bang amazed the large crowd.   ....

   William is rude and untidy at home.   ....

   Claire enjoyed the old, scary book.   ....

   The toddlers were tired and grumpy.   ....

   2 marks

Adjectives

4) Circle all the adjectives in the box below.

> tiny   straight   helpful   immense   skinny
> always   lively   never   dry   hardly
> joyful   business

2 marks

5) Complete the table of adjectives below.

Adjective	Comparative	Superlative
fast	faster	fastest
quiet	....	....
....	angrier	....
gentle	....	....

2 marks

6) Rewrite these sentences, replacing the adjectives with more interesting ones.

The hotel had a <u>good</u> pool and a <u>good</u> restaurant with <u>good</u> staff.

....

....

Emily is <u>kind</u> and Ivan is <u>kind</u>, but Philip is not very <u>kind</u>.

....

....

2 marks

How would you describe your adjective skills, young Grammagator? Are you wonderful, or working on it?

Adverbs

Adverbs describe verbs, adjectives and other adverbs. Here's some handy practice on them.

1) Join each adverb (white box) with the most appropriate verb (grey box).

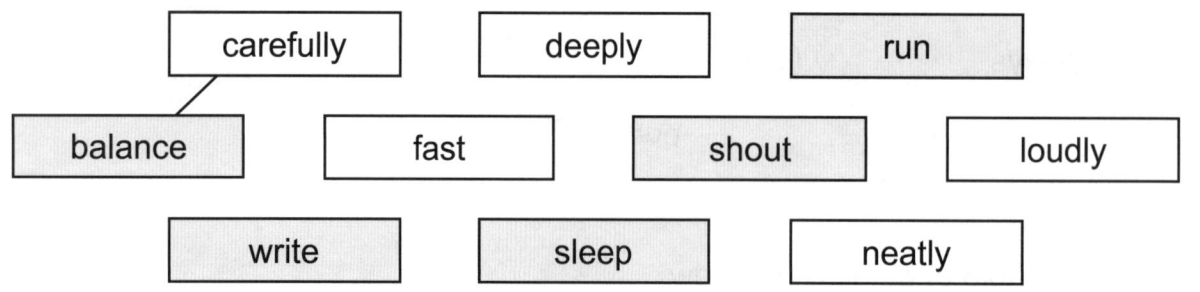

2 marks

2) Add your own adverbs to these sentences to describe the underlined verbs.

Mr Lawrence <u>waved</u> to his neighbour, who <u>scowled</u> and <u>walked</u> away.

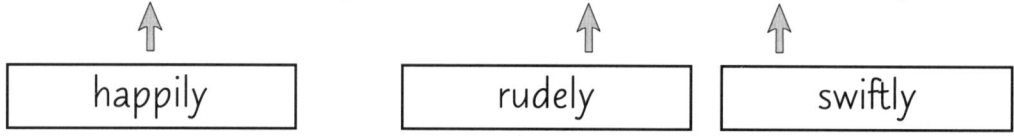

Dinah <u>stared</u> out the classroom window, <u>sighing</u> and <u>wishing</u> she was outside.

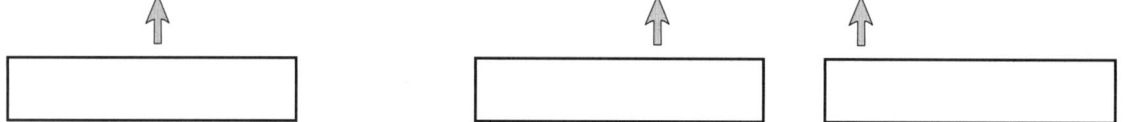

As the crowd <u>cheered</u>, I <u>grabbed</u> the ladder and began to <u>climb</u>.

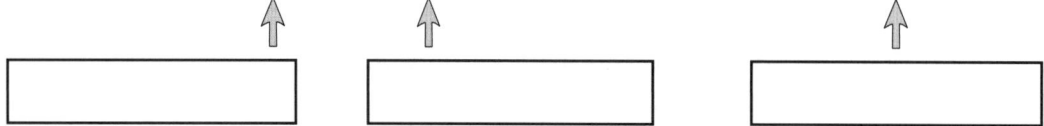

2 marks

3) Turn these adjectives into adverbs.

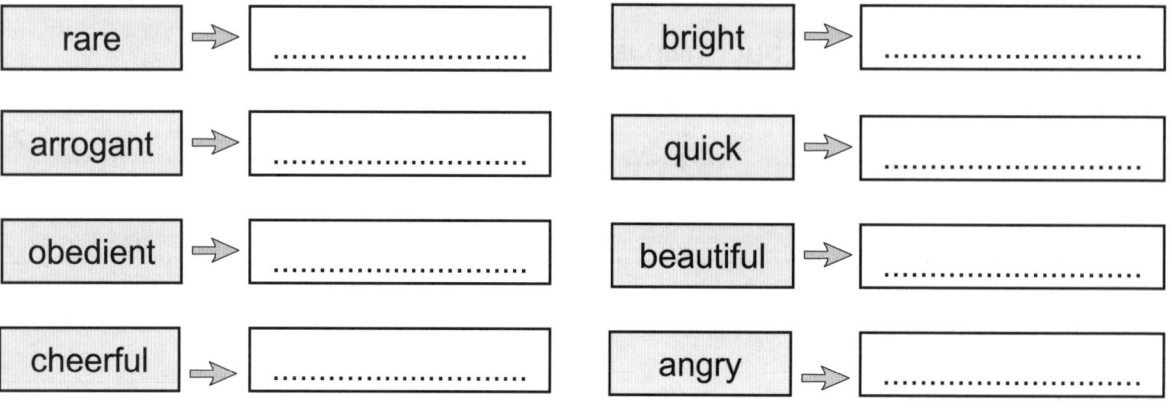

2 marks

Section 1 — Types of Word

Adverbs

4) Complete the sentences with adverbs from the box. Use each adverb once.

| next | never | after | sometimes | soon |

After school, I do my homework, and I play football shortly ....

Sabrina and I get on really well — we .... argue.

I had seen the film before, so I knew what was going to happen ....

He's not here at the moment, but he will .... arrive.

The school bus is usually on time, but .... it's late.

2 marks

5) Circle the adverb that fits the sentence best.

Percy the pony is over (**there / somewhere**), nibbling a carrot.

She had travelled the world and had (**there / nowhere**) else to visit.

You haven't cleaned the house for weeks — there is dust (**everywhere / here**).

When the river flooded, the water came right up to (**somewhere / here**).

2 marks

6) Underline the **two** adverbs in each sentence below.

"Surely you can't be serious!" shouted Petunia angrily.

This sculpture is incredibly valuable; therefore we must be careful with it.

We will probably need to finish the painting soon.

Perhaps I should ask Natalia since she speaks Russian fluently.

2 marks

Grammagators handle adverbs as coolly as a cucumber.
Tick a box to show how well you did with these pages.

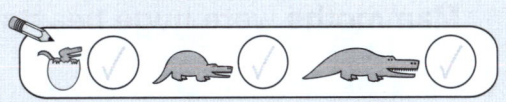

© CGP — not to be photocopied

Section 1 — Types of Word

Mixed practice

Congratulations — you've reached the end of Section 1! That was a lot of practice. It's time to bring together everything you've learnt so far. Ready, set, Grammagator...

1) Circle the two common nouns and underline the two verbs in each sentence.

   The CD installed, and the game loaded straight away.

   I know that the parrot stole my diary.

   2 marks

2) Draw a line from each sentence to the correct word type to identify the word in bold.

   Zahra wore her **green** dress.   determiner   **You** look much better.

   We soon put out **the** flames.   Maurice is a **fierce** lion.

                                            pronoun

   Eva bought **a** bun for May.   Zotia had **some** eggs.

   He wouldn't stop talking.   adjective   Dad beat **me** at cards.

   2 marks

3) Underline all the adverbs in the sentence below.

   We must finish this lovely mosaic soon; therefore we must work quickly.

   2 marks

4) Write the appropriate possessive pronoun to complete each sentence.

   The hamster belongs to Priyan and Maria — it's ....

   Simon sold his bike to me — now it's ....

   You and Peter own this donkey — it's ....

   2 marks

5) Underline all the adjectives in the sentence below.

   Mammoths were huge beasts with thick, hairy coats and long tusks.

   2 marks

Section 1 — Types of Word

Mixed practice

6) Rewrite this sentence, replacing the underlined adverb with a **more** certain adverb.

   I will <u>probably</u> spend my pocket money on a new train set.

   ....

   ....

   1 mark

7) Write the correct plural for each singular noun.

mouse ⇒	woman ⇒ ....
church ⇒	baby ⇒ ....
leaf ⇒	school ⇒ ....

   2 marks

8) Write a sentence that uses the word **answer** as a **verb**.

   ....

   ....

   Write a sentence that uses the word **answer** as a **noun**.

   ....

   ....

   2 marks

9) Choose an appropriate adverb to go in the space in each of these sentences.

   Jamie behaved .... at the birthday meal.

   The waiter .... spilt the coffee over my dad.

   The cat looked .... at the little blackbird.

   2 marks

Mixed practice

10) Tick the version of each sentence which uses verbs correctly.

Camille makes beautiful cards. ☐   Camille make beautiful cards. ☐

We buys our fruit at the market. ☐   We buy our fruit at the market. ☐

My uncle was very tired. ☐   My uncle were very tired. ☐

They does extreme sports. ☐   They do extreme sports. ☐

2 marks

11) Match each label below to the correct word in the sentence.

The swarm of angry bees (attacked) Leonie.

| adjective | verb | collective noun | proper noun |

The chief needed all his courage to bravely fight the bears.

| singular noun | adverb | abstract noun | plural noun |

Juan and Hélène have sneakily taken my bin because theirs is broken.

| determiner | adverb | possessive pronoun | adjective |

We should plant the roses over there.

| plural noun | pronoun | adverb | modal verb |

2 marks

12) You might not recognise the word below in **bold**, but explain how you can tell it's a proper noun.

Lots of tourists travel to **Heidelberg** each year.

....

1 mark

Section 1 — Types of Word   © CGP — not to be photocopied

Mixed practice

13) Cross out the incorrect form of the verb in the sentences below.

The king (**has / have**) a hundred servants.   Ty (**go / goes**) skiing every year.

Dai and Kirsty (**comes / come**) round often.   This lollipop (**is / are**) delicious.

We always (**do / does**) the crossword.   My aunt (**write / writes**) letters.

2 marks

14) Underline the error in each sentence, and write the correction in the space.

The shelfs fell off the wall an hour later.   ⇒   ....

Dad bought me a iced bun as a treat.   ⇒   ....

Adam and me went for a walk on Tuesday.   ⇒   ....

2 marks

15) Write a sentence that includes a **modal verb**, an **adverb** and a **collective noun**. Then, write your words on the dotted lines below.

....

....

modal verb: ....   **adverb:** ....   **collective noun:** ....

Write a sentence that includes a **possessive pronoun**, an **adjective** and a **determiner**. Then, write your words on the dotted lines below.

....

....

possessive pronoun: ....   **adjective:** ....   **determiner:** ....

2 marks

Phew! That was a serious grammar workout. How are you feeling after Section One? Are you a Grammagator?

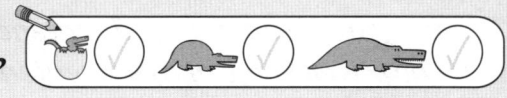

Section 2 — Clauses, Phrases and Sentences

Sentences

Sentences need to make sense. Don't get tense — just make them make sense.

1) Match each sentence to the correct label on the right.

   I sometimes sing in the shower. ——— Makes sense

   They said that they knew the.

   Mark knows can do it. Doesn't make sense

   Let's go to the cinema.

   2 marks

2) Put an 'S' in each box after a statement and a 'C' in each box after a command.

   Turn off the television and give the remote to me. ☐

   When you're in the park, you must keep your dog on a lead at all times. ☐

   I don't want you to come in yet because the display isn't ready. ☐

   2 marks

3) Using all the words in the box, complete these sentences so they make sense.

   | plays   out   we   present |

   After dinner, ... told ghost stories around the fire.

   I gave Konstantin a .... on his birthday.

   Harriet .... badminton every Tuesday.

   The baker took the loaf of bread .... of the oven.

   2 marks

Grammagators sense a good sentence. Tick the box to show how well you can make sentences make sense.

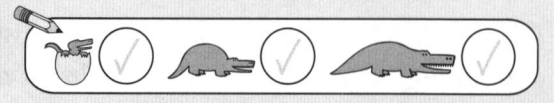

Section 2 — Clauses, Phrases and Sentences

Paragraphs

Paragraphs break up chunks of text. So, hammers out, and let's get cracking...

1) Read this piece of text, and mark with a // where new paragraphs should begin. There are <u>nine</u> paragraphs in total.

   Daniel heard a thump. It was definitely a thump, and it came from under his bed. "What's going on up there?" his mum called up the stairs. "Nothing," Daniel hastily replied. The night before, Daniel had heard a similar noise, but he had been too scared to take a look. It was dark under his bed, and he was worried about what he might find. At Tim's house, for example, Tim's sister found an enormous spider under her bed. She says it's not true that spiders have eight legs — the one she discovered had at least twenty. "Pull yourself together," Daniel whispered to himself as he grabbed the edge of the bed, ready to tip himself upside down to investigate. With one quick movement, Daniel faced the darkness, but kept his eyes closed. What happened next was worse than he'd expected — Daniel was attacked by a long, warm, slimy object that flew about his face, leaving streaks of slobber behind. The beast then advanced towards Daniel with a squeal, knocking him to the floor and scrabbling over his body to reach his face once more. After a short while, Daniel began to giggle. His giggle soon turned into fits of laughter, and he started to roll around the floor. "Oh Molly, you silly dog — it's only you!" he cried.

   2 marks

2) Write down three different reasons why you started some of your paragraphs in question 1.

   ....

   ....

   ....

   3 marks

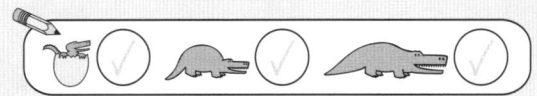

Grammagators like to break text up into tasty chunks.
Tick the box to show how well you use paragraphs.

Phrases

A phrase is part of a sentence that never has both a verb and a subject — sometimes it has neither. See if you can spot the phrases that pop up in the questions below.

1) Write a 'P' in the boxes next to any options below which are phrases.

   they are happy ☐   as soon as possible ☐

   I don't like ham ☐   we train hard ☐

   fancy cake cases ☐   our history teacher ☐

   rather confusing ☐   despite the rain ☐

   Jim builds sheds ☐   he counts in French ☐

   on Saturday night ☐   unlimited chocolate ☐

   2 marks

2) Underline the adverbials in the sentences below.

   The lorry made its way up the hill exceedingly slowly.

   Walter and Lucinda play the castanets most skilfully.

   It is highly unlikely that you will find a water buffalo in your garden pond.

   Cho applied the brakes, but the train was still moving dangerously fast.

   > An adverbial is a word or phrase that's used like an adverb. It gives more information about a verb or clause.

   2 marks

3) Underline the prepositional phrase in each of these sentences.

   We need to get the horse <u>out of the kitchen</u>.

   The walkers ended up lost in the middle of nowhere.

   After school, I play football and walk the dog.

   We left before lunch, and we didn't return.

   > A preposition tells you where or when something is in relation to other things.

   2 marks

Section 2 — Clauses, Phrases and Sentences   © CGP — not to be photocopied

Phrases

4) Underline the noun phrases in the sentences below.

The angry man chased his big brother down the road.

The fire-breathing dragon escaped from the wizard's castle.

A noun phrase is a group of words that includes a noun. In a sentence, noun phrases behave like nouns.

The old oak tree came crashing down on top of the flowers.

My friend Albert found a prickly hedgehog in his back garden.

2 marks

5) Complete the sentences below by adding a fronted adverbial.

.... , my sister and I went to the new museum.

.... , Amy is going to drive all the way to Bath.

.... , Nish is building a den in the back garden.

2 marks

6) Rewrite the sentences below, replacing the underlined parts with a shorter noun phrase that has the same meaning. The first one has been done for you.

The kitten was rescued from the tree by <u>the hero who was strong and fearless</u>.

The kitten was rescued from the tree by the strong and fearless hero.

The house I live in has <u>a living room which is small but cosy</u>.

....

The ship was taken over by <u>pirates who were mean and grumpy</u>.

....

2 marks

Phrases are the bread and butter of sentences for all good Grammagators. Are you happy with phrases?

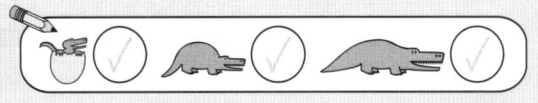

Clauses

A clause is a bit of a sentence that contains both a subject and a verb — they're pretty greedy.

1) In the table below, tick to show whether the bold words are phrases or clauses.

Sentence	Phrase	Clause
Jim and Julie go dancing every other afternoon.		
Our family goes to Wales **during the holidays**.		
Merlin completed the test **incredibly quickly**.		
The children played out in the fresh air.		

2 marks

2) Match each clause to the correct label below.

I am on my way to Manchester

although I don't like pork pies

because the sun is shining

they're determined to win

despite what they say

main clause

subordinate clause

2 marks

3) Underline the main clause in each of these sentences.

Since it was Christine's birthday, <u>Tony made her breakfast in bed</u>.

> You can tell that this is the main clause because it makes sense on its own.

Joanne kept eating sweets until the bag was empty.

Granny and Grandpa will take us to the park if there's time.

While you tickle the cat, I'll shampoo the parrot.

2 marks

Section 2 — Clauses, Phrases and Sentences

Clauses

4) Tick the sentences that contain a subordinate clause, and underline the subordinate clauses.

I was late for work because my car broke down. ☐

My car broke down, and I was late for work. ☐

When my car broke down, I was late for work. ☐

Subordinate clauses don't make sense on their own — they have to be joined to a main clause.

2 marks

5) Make each pair of sentences below into one sentence, making sure that each sentence contains a main clause and a subordinate clause.
Underline the subordinate clause in your answer.

E.g. Mary went to the shop. She needed to buy some milk.
Mary went to the shop <u>because she needed to buy some milk</u>.

It was raining. We played tennis.

....

I chopped the carrots. My sister chopped the parsnips.

....

....

2 marks

6) Write a subordinate clause for each of these sentences.

.... , she set off to the park.

We would have missed the bus ....

The elephants were very happy ....

.... , they still had fun.

2 marks

Grammagators are sharp when it comes to clauses.
Can you spot different clauses too? Tick a box.

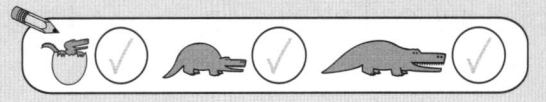

© CGP — not to be photocopied

Relative clauses

A relative clause is a subordinate clause that often starts with a relative pronoun. Relative pronouns are words like 'who', 'that', 'which', 'whom' and 'whose'.

1) Tick the sentences that contain a relative clause, and then underline the relative clauses.

   Anyone who wants to join in must be in the playground at 3.30 pm. ☐

   The teddy bear race, which takes place every year, was a big success. ☐

   I went to the party with Marie, whose brother is my new best friend. ☐

   Lars was not sure when the country fair was going to take place. ☐

   My parents have just moved out of the house where I grew up. ☐

   2 marks

2) Cross out the incorrect relative pronoun in the sentences below.

   The Smiths, (**who / which**) live next door, have painted their house blue.

   A washing line, (**who / which**) is one mile long, is attracting a lot of attention.

   Eileen, (**whom / whose**) brother lives in France, is captain of the football team.

   The vegetable patch is the part of the garden (**that / who**) I like best.

   I'm not sure (**whose / whom**) coat that is, but it looks like the one Phillip lost.

   2 marks

3) Complete the sentences below by adding a relative pronoun in the space.

   Tyrone, ... loves to play squash, has joined the local sports club.

   The treacle tart was the dessert .... tasted the most delicious.

   I want to go back to the stadium .... has a blue roof.

   I invited Lorraine, ... I met at karate club, over for tea.

   2 marks

Section 2 — Clauses, Phrases and Sentences

Relative clauses

4) Put a tick in the boxes to show which relative pronouns could be removed from the sentences below. Make sure the sentences still make sense.

The TV show which I'm watching (the one which discusses animals) is great.

⇧ ☐   ⇧ ☐

Carol's sister, who is very clever, has read the book that I'm studying at school.

⇧ ☐   ⇧ ☐

2 marks

5) Choose a relative clause from the boxes below, and write a sentence using that relative clause. Remember to add commas where they are needed.

| who stared at me | which was expensive | that I saw on Sunday |

....

....

1 mark

6) Write a relative clause for each of these sentences.

Victor is the police officer ....

That's the house ....

Mrs Potter is the dinner lady ....

Badal gave me a present ....

2 marks

Relative clauses are as friendly as your closest relatives. Do you agree? Tick to show your level.

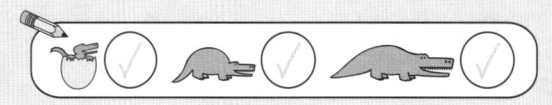

© CGP — not to be photocopied

Section 2 — Clauses, Phrases and Sentences

Mixed practice

It's time to mix things up. These four pages of mixed practice take a look back at Section 2. Have a go at all the questions, and see how well you do. Remember to tick a box on page 31.

1) Write down whether each sentence is a statement, question or command.

   There's an ice cream van parked outside ....

   Take the next turning on the left ....

   Where is the nearest post office ....

   Do you think fish scones will taste nice ....

   2 marks

2) Using all of the adjectives in the box, rewrite the noun phrases below, adding two adjectives to each phrase.

ferocious	cute	talkative	cuddly	chirpy	mean

   a dog ....

   the kitten ....

   parrots ....

   2 marks

3) Underline the noun phrase in each of these sentences.
   Then rewrite the sentence, replacing the noun phrase with the correct pronoun.

   My big brother drives slowly. ....

   Where are the cherry cookies? ....

   The pink balloon is missing. ....

   A new sweet shop has opened. ....

   Can Beth's aunty come? ....

   2 marks

Section 2 — Clauses, Phrases and Sentences

Mixed practice

4) Underline the subordinate clause in each of these sentences.

Juliet began to cry <u>because Romeo left her</u>. ← You can tell that this is the subordinate clause because it doesn't make sense on its own.

When I'm older, I would love to live in America.

Before she went to bed, she read her book.

You'll miss the train if you don't leave now.

2 marks

5) Write down whether each phrase is an adverbial (A) or a noun phrase (N).

a small panda	A	more dangerously	☐
my untidy bedroom	☐	the distant mountains	☐
the lovely garden	☐	really joyfully	☐
very bravely	☐	your cuddly kitten	☐
ten hungry badgers	☐	incredibly quickly	☐
reasonably quietly	☐	far too slowly	☐

2 marks

6) Write a main clause for each sentence below, and add a comma if necessary.

If there's a problem ....

.... because I was angry.

Whilst I cleaned up ....

.... unless it's a secret.

Although Tom tried his best ....

2 marks

Mixed practice

7) Using all of the words below, fill in the gaps in this text so that it makes sense.

| melted | mix | chocolate | pour | mug | perfect |

To make the .... hot chocolate, you will need 35 g of chocolate and 250 ml of semi-skimmed milk. .... the milk into a pan, and warm it over a medium heat. Meanwhile, break the .... into pieces, and add the pieces to the pan. .... the milk and the chocolate with a wooden spoon until the chocolate pieces have .... Turn off the heat, and carefully pour the hot chocolate into a .... Serve with whipped cream, mini marshmallows and a generous helping of chocolate sprinkles. Sit back and enjoy!

2 marks

8) Tick the sentences that would still make sense without a relative pronoun.

The bag that I use for my P.E. kit gets very smelly. ☐

There was a cloud of smoke which filled the kitchen. ☐

We met the prince who is going to be king one day. ☐

I know the place that you're talking about. ☐

2 marks

9) Underline the relative clause in each of these sentences.

Colin works for a company which makes chocolate biscuits.

Henry introduced me to the woman who judges the baking contest.

2 marks

10) Write a relative clause for each of these sentences.

I bought the car ....

Yesterday, I saw the man ....

2 marks

Section 2 — Clauses, Phrases and Sentences

Mixed practice

11) Read this piece of text, and mark where new paragraphs should begin with //. There are six paragraphs in total.

At the side of the lagoon in Hognose Valley, the Humbletons were sitting by the campfire, stewing their dinner of wriggly eels. The Humbletons were curious creatures — their noses were black, their feet were webbed, and their hair was pondweed green. Over in a neighbouring valley lived the Poggleworths. Like the Humbletons, the Poggleworths were also fond of eels, but that's where their similarities ended. In fact, these two clans didn't get on at all. It all began two hundred years ago when the leader of the Poggleworths forbade his daughter from marrying a Humbleton squire. "If you go against my wishes," he said, "You will not be welcome here." The Humbleton leader learnt of this and was furious. He declared war on the Poggleworths, and a bitter fight broke out which lasted many months. Eventually, the fighting ceased, but the battle was never forgotten.

2 marks

12) Complete the sentences below by adding a relative clause in the space. Remember to add commas where they're needed.

The spelling test .... was really tricky.

Our postman .... won't deliver parcels.

Jonathan's bedroom .... needs a clean.

2 marks

13) Draw lines to match the options below to the correct label.

| I went swimming | subordinate clause |

| on Tuesday at 9.30 am | main clause |

| because it was cold | phrase |

2 marks

Grammagators like a bit of variety.
How well did you do with this mixture of questions?

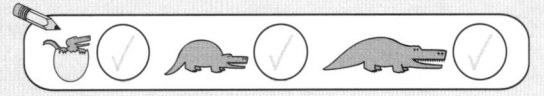

Section 3 — Conjunctions and Prepositions

Co-ordinating conjunctions

Conjunctions are words that link clauses in a sentence. Co-ordinating conjunctions link two main clauses, phrases or words that are equally important.

1) Underline the co-ordinating conjunctions in the sentences below.

   Melanie likes to play netball <u>and</u> cricket. *This coordinating conjunction tells you that Melanie likes playing netball and cricket equally.*

   Laura paints murals, but she prefers to make jewellery.

   Kamini was late for work, so she began to run.

   Penguins don't eat sandwiches, nor do they eat ice cream.

   2 marks

2) Using the co-ordinating conjunctions in the box, complete the sentences below.

and	nor	but	or	so

   Use each conjunction only once.

   We could either watch a film, ... we could play a board game.

   It began to rain really hard, ... we got very wet.

   The brownies were good, ... the muffins were even better.

   Sam doesn't go swimming, ... does he go cycling.

   Oliver is going to the bank, ... then he is going to buy a piano.

   2 marks

3) Join this pair of sentences using a co-ordinating conjunction.

   I was really thirsty.   I drank a glass of orange squash.

   ....

   1 mark

Co-ordinating conjunctions might sound scary, but Grammagators are brave. How did this page go?

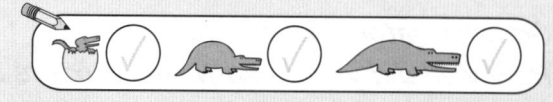

Section 3 — Conjunctions and Prepositions

Subordinating conjunctions

Subordinating conjunctions join subordinate clauses to main clauses.

1) Underline the most suitable subordinating conjunctions in the passage below.

   Ashley and Jason are twins, (**although** / **because**) they don't have much in common, and their hobbies are very different. Ashley likes to go to salsa classes, (**if** / **whereas**) Jason prefers skateboarding.

   (**Although** / **Whenever**) skateboarding can be dangerous, Jason practises complicated tricks (**until** / **unless**) he finally gets them right (**while** / **since**) he enjoys showing new skills to his friends.

   (**Whereas** / **While**) Ashley is dancing, she forgets all her troubles, so she feels much better after each session.

   (**Even though** / **So that**) they have different interests, Ashley and Jason rarely argue and manage to get along most of the time.

   2 marks

2) The sentence below is incorrect. Rewrite it using an appropriate subordinating conjunction.

   My hamster has been acting strangely unless he ate those mysterious berries.

   ....

   ....

   1 mark

3) Join up the correct parts of the sentences so that they make sense.

My dog ate the steak	when	I wasn't looking.
I was very full	while	the balloons popped.
Wojtek was startled	unless	I had eaten too much.
I'm not going	because	you come with me.

   2 marks

Grammagators like subordinating conjunctions even though they can be tricky. How did you find them?

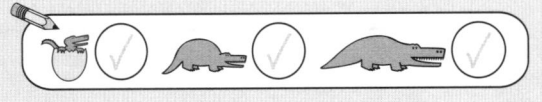

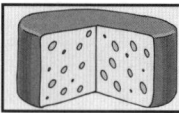

Prepositions

Prepositions tell you how things are related in a sentence. Oh, look — more questions!

1) Circle the prepositions below.

since, revolting, across, next to, age, thundering, behind, around, closely, onto, superb, because of, at, nearly

2 marks

2) Cross out the incorrect preposition in each sentence.

I have a haircut (**at / on**) eleven o'clock.

I try to drink water (**within / throughout**) the day.

The dog dived (**during / into**) the swimming pool.

2 marks

3) Sort the prepositions in the box below into the correct column.

~~over~~, during, until, inside, upon, before, after, in front of

when something happens	where something happens
....	.... over ....
....	....
....	....
....	....

2 marks

Prepositions

4) Join up the correct parts of the sentences so that they make sense.

Edward was hiding	because of	the double bed.
Mark spilt the lemonade	underneath	the heavy rain.
The pitch was very wet	since	my favourite toy.
We have been waiting	over	six o'clock.

2 marks

5) Rewrite the sentence below with different prepositions to replace the words in bold. Don't worry if the meaning of the sentence changes.

Turn right **after** the traffic lights, then go **under** the bridge **by** the station.

....

....

2 marks

6) Write two sentences explaining how you get to school from your home. Use at least **three** prepositions in your answer, and underline them.

....

....

....

2 marks

7) In the boxes below, write whether the word in bold is a **preposition** (P) or an **adverb** (A).

Remember — adverbs describe verbs, adjectives and other adverbs.

The rollercoaster sped **up**. ☐   Katie ran **up** the stairs. ☐

I dropped it **down** the well. ☐   Dad told me to get **down**. ☐

2 marks

Are you ahead of the game on prepositions, or do you need some more practice? Tick a box, Grammagator.

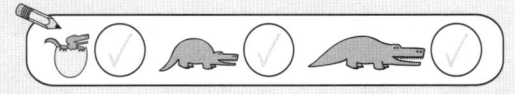

Mixed practice

It's time to mix things up with an assortment of practice questions. Have a go at all these questions, and see how well you know your conjunctions and prepositions.

1) In the boxes below, write whether each word is a **co-ordinating conjunction** (C) or a **subordinating conjunction** (S).

   if ☐   when ☐   yet ☐   whereas ☐   because ☐

   while ☐   since ☐   or ☐   nor ☐   but ☐

   2 marks

2) Underline the prepositions in the sentences below.

   Kimberly hid under the table while Loretta looked for her behind the curtains.

   The magician marched onto the stage and instantly fell through the trapdoor.

   I went into the sitting room and sat opposite my sister.

   The alien spaceship landed behind my house, next to the pond.

   2 marks

3) Join the beginning and end of each sentence using the correct co-ordinating conjunction.

Beginning of Sentence	Conjunction	End of Sentence
Jean went to the gym,	or	they didn't have eggs.
They wanted pancakes,	and	Ted went to the shop.
He can either play darts	so	I can't go swimming.
I have a bad cold,	but	snooker.

   2 marks

4) In the boxes below, write whether the word in bold is being used as a **preposition** (P) or a **subordinating conjunction** (SC).

   We'll call you **before** we set off. ☐   She has been jogging **since** 8 am. ☐

   Flo watched a film **after** school. ☐   He won't leave **until** he's finished. ☐

   2 marks

Mixed practice

5) Underline all the conjunctions in the passage below.

I was upset because my sister had stolen my favourite train set. I asked her to give it back, but she just ignored me and carried on playing with it. When our parents came home, she still wouldn't give the train set back, even though they told her to.

2 marks

6) Link these pairs of sentences using a co-ordinating conjunction.
Use a different conjunction each time.

My hamster escaped from his cage.   I quickly caught him again.

....

....

Jimmy will either move to Paris.   He will move to Moscow.

....

....

2 marks

7) Tick the version of each sentence which uses the correct preposition.

I put the pizza into the oven. ☐   I put the pizza from the oven. ☐

The kangaroo stood at me. ☐   The kangaroo stood beside me. ☐

Brian put the pie on the table. ☐   Brian put the pie into the table. ☐

He climbed through the window. ☐   He climbed since the window. ☐

2 marks

8) Write a sentence with a subordinating conjunction. Circle the conjunction.

....

1 mark

*Grammagators think that variety is the spice of life.
How well did you do with this mixture of questions?*

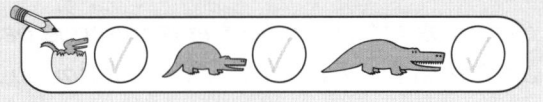

Section 4 — Sentence Structure and Tense

Subject and object

A subject is the person or thing doing the verb. An object has something done to it. Let's see how you get on with these questions about subjects and objects.

1) Underline the subject in each of the sentences below.

   The stag stood on top of the hill. He tells a lot of great jokes.

   Martin gave Danielle a kiss. Filip and Tom are in Greece.

   A spaceship flew around the Earth. The police officer frowned.

   The weather seems to be improving. My dog chased Atul's cat.

   2 marks

2) Look the options below. Write an 'S' in the box when the underlined part is the subject and an 'O' in the box when the underlined part is the object.

   Yvonne covered <u>Gary's hair</u> with shaving foam. ☐

   <u>The children</u> persuaded the teacher to do a dance. ☐

   On Tuesday, <u>Gudrun</u> gave her rabbits extra carrots. ☐

   2 marks

3) Underline the object in each of the sentences below. Then rewrite each sentence, replacing the object with your own object. The first one has been done for you.

   Sally and Lilly welcomed <u>the visitors</u>.

   Sally and Lilly welcomed Roger. ← 'the visitors' (a plural object) has been replaced with 'Roger' (a singular object).

   He saw a chimney sweep on the roof.

   ....

   Kareem met Nancy at the bus stop.

   ....

   2 marks

Grammagators know the difference between subjects and objects. Do you? Tick the box to show how you did.

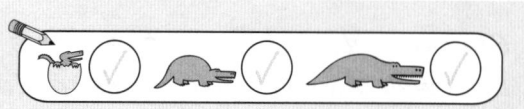

Active and passive voice

An active sentence has a subject that does something.
In passive sentences, something is done to the subject.

1) Draw lines to show whether each sentence is active or passive.

   The jewels sparkled in the moonlight.

   The roof was damaged in the strong winds.

   The waiter served the first course.

   The damaged costumes were quickly repaired.

   The prisoners escaped by digging their way out.

   active

   passive

   2 marks

2) Rearrange these words to form a passive sentence.

   the   awarded   were   they   prize   first   mayor   by

   ....

   Now rewrite the sentence as an active sentence.

   ....

   2 marks

3) Rewrite this active sentence as a passive sentence.

   Uncle Max caught the chickens.

   ....

   1 mark

4) Rewrite this passive sentence as an active sentence.

   Mary was chased by Tina.

   ....

   1 mark

You need to get active and practise this stuff for your SATs. Tick the box to show how well you know it.

Past, present and future tenses

The past tense shows that something has finished. The present tense shows what's happening now or what happens regularly. The future tense shows what will happen.

1) Write whether each sentence below is in the past, present or future tense.

   The "-ed" ending on the verb 'injured' tells you that it happened in the past.

   I inju(red) my leg in a rugby match. ....past.................

   Yusef will wait by the gate. ....

   My earplugs drowned out the noise. ....

   I keep my coloured pencils in a tin. ....

   We will finish our homework later. ....

   Everyone was frightened by the film. ....

   2 marks

2) Complete the table below with the correct forms of these verbs.

Past	Present
....	I carry
Hamish opened	....
We hurried	....
....	It itches
....	They follow
She shook	....

   2 marks

3) Underline all the verbs in the sentences below.
   Then rewrite the sentences in the past tense on the lines below.

   I go into local schools and teach piano lessons. I also play the oboe.

   ....

   ....

   2 marks

Section 4 — Sentence Structure and Tense © CGP — not to be photocopied

Past, present and future tenses

4) Choose the correct form of the verb to complete the sentences. Use each option once.

Edward .... his chores yesterday.

I always .... my best at trampolining club.

The pupils have .... all of their homework.

Jenny .... better paintings than me.

do

does

done

did

2 marks

5) Rewrite this sentence using the correct verb from the brackets.

If he wants to pass the exam, he (**can / will**) need to study hard.

....

1 mark

6) Rewrite these sentences in the future tense.
Aliens came to Earth and took over the planet. They were very powerful.

....

....

2 marks

7) Tick the sentences that use verb tenses correctly.

The doctor took my pulse and listens to my chest. ☐

I cycle to school in summer and take the bus in winter. ☐

I hope we will see you again soon to continued our chat. ☐

Tomek hates spinach, but he loves spaghetti. ☐

We posted the cards on Tuesday, but they haven't arrived. ☐

2 marks

Grammagators don't get tense about verb tenses. They know all about them. Tick a box to show your level.

Verbs with 'have'

The present perfect uses 'have' to talk about something that happened recently.

1) Tick the sentences below that use the present perfect.

   Saeed went to play in the park. ☐

   The fence has been broken for a long time. ☐

   The Johnsons have decided to sell their car. ☐

   2 marks

2) Complete the sentences below by adding '**have**' or '**has**'.

   I .... just got back from a holiday in Yorkshire.

   Riley .... told me that if he wins, he'll get a medal.

   We .... bought a rug that will match the sofa.

   The police .... already surrounded the building.

   She .... changed her mind about going to the beach.

   2 marks

3) Rewrite these sentences using the present perfect.

   Larry decided to join the circus.

   ..... Larry has decided to join the circus. ....

   The man gave the dog a bone.

   ....

   Marek and John went to the park.

   ....

   2 marks

How did you get on with these questions? Did you find them easy? Tick to show how you performed.

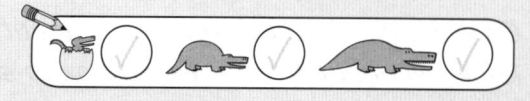

Section 4 — Sentence Structure and Tense © CGP — not to be photocopied

Verbs with '-ing'

It's time to take a look at verbs with '-ing'. Let's see how you do with these questions.

1) Rewrite these sentences using the present tense with '-ing'. The first one has been done for you.

   The present tense with '-ing' is sometimes called the 'present progressive' or the 'present continuous'.

   Marcus plays tennis.   Marcus is playing tennis.

   Tariq takes me home.   ....

   They wash up.   ....

   I travel by train.   ....

   The pupils think.   ....

   2 marks

2) Cross out the incorrect words to form the **past tense** with '-ing'.

   The past tense with '-ing' is sometimes called the 'past progressive' or the 'past continuous'.

   The problem (**is / was / are**) (**get / getting / gets**) worse.

   Bea's cats (**are / were / is**) (**chasing / chased / chase**) a bird.

   She (**is / are / was**) (**chopped / chopping / chops**) the vegetables.

   My shoes (**are / was / were**) (**squash / squashed / squashing**) my toes.

   2 marks

3) Use the words in the box to write your own sentences in the **present tense** with '-ing'.

   | laugh | begin | run |

   ....

   ....

   ....

   2 marks

Are you a Grammagator who knows all about using verbs with '-ing'? Tick a box to show how well you did.

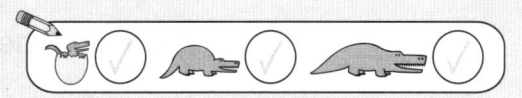

Mixed practice

You've reached the end of Section 4. Now it's time to see how great you are at sentence structures and tenses. These exercises will test all of the topics in this section. Go get 'em...

1) Rewrite the sentence below in the **future** tense.

   I keep baby dinosaurs in my room, and I feed them toast and jam.

   ....

   ....

   Rewrite the sentence below in the **past** tense.

   I forget my P.E. kit and lose my pencil, so my teacher is cross with me.

   ....

   ....

   2 marks

2) Underline the verb in each sentence that is incorrect.
   Write the correct form on the line.

   They play nicely together and takes turns.   ....

   John like chocolate, but he hates sweets.   ....

   She boils the eggs and fry the sausages.   ....

   I know Sarah very well, and I trusts her.   ....

   We grow vegetables and plants lots of seeds.   ....

   2 marks

3) Complete the sentences below by adding '**have**' or '**has**'.

   Brian .... built an amazing sandcastle on the beach.

   The bus .... broken down, so I am going to be late.

   You .... challenged me to a duel, and I accept.

   2 marks

Section 4 — Sentence Structure and Tense © CGP — not to be photocopied

Mixed practice

4) Complete each sentence by writing in a subject.

.... hid under the bed.

.... has an impressive view of the sea.

.... are arguing with the police officer.

2 marks

5) Circle the subject in each sentence below.
   Then complete each sentence by writing in an object.

   Liam and Lucas pretended they couldn't see ....

   My train overtook .... at top speed.

   Boris warned .... about the hole in the garden.

2 marks

6) Look at the options below. Write an 'A' in the box next to the active sentence and a 'P' in the box next to the passive sentence.

   The birds wake me up every morning. ☐

   I am woken up by the birds every morning. ☐

2 marks

7) Complete the table using the correct form of 'to be' and the '-ing' form of each verb. The first line has been done for you.

verb	present tense	past tense
go	Harvey ...is going... to school.	Harvey ...was going... to school.
try	We .... to do it.	We .... to do it.
pop	My ears	My ears ....
write	They .... a letter.	They .... a letter.
fall	The tower .... down.	The tower .... down.

2 marks

Wow, that was a whole lot of practice! Do you feel like the leader of the Grammagators now? Tick a box.

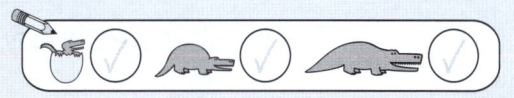

Section 5 — Writing Style

Standard vs. Non-Standard

Standard English follows normal spelling, punctuation and grammar rules. It's a more formal type of English. Let's give it a whirl.

1) Match up each sentence on the left with the correct label on the right.

   "*doesn't* want *no*" is a double negative.

   - He doesn't want no dinner. → Non-Standard English
   - He couldn't do anything to help.
   - I haven't got no pets.
   - You can't do nothing to stop me.

   Standard English

   Non-Standard English

   2 marks

2) Underline the words which show that the sentences below are in Non-Standard English, and then rewrite each sentence in Standard English.

   Tai's gonna speak to Mr Smith. ....

   I won't of left by then. ....

   She ain't happy about it. ....

   There's the dog what I like. ....

   2 marks

3) Draw lines to show which word completes these sentences in Standard English.

   .... went to the park after school.

   Polly and .... had an argument.

   James gave .... a present.

   Maria and .... are learning Greek.

   The teacher was angry with Martin and ....

   I

   me

   2 marks

Standard vs. Non-Standard

4) Complete the sentences below using '**good**' or '**well**'.

Leo did .... in his exam.

She repaired it very ....

The play was surprisingly ....

He got a .... mark overall.

2 marks

5) Cross out the incorrect option so that each sentence is in Standard English.

(**We are building / We is building**) a treehouse.

Every week, (**he go / he goes**) to the zoo.

(**They has / They have**) loads of money.

In Standard English, the subject and the verb need to agree — they should both be singular or both be plural.

(**The camel were / The camel was**) really grumpy.

Despite the rain, (**they were / they was**) in a good mood.

2 marks

6) Complete the sentences below using '**them**' or '**those**'.

When we went to the beach, I had one of .... lovely ice lollies.

Sarah usually goes to visit .... on her way home from school.

George loves .... purple trousers, but Thomas prefers the green ones.

2 marks

7) Rewrite each sentence below in Standard English.

Karen drived really quick. ....

I were riding my bike to school. ....

Helen has wrote a letter. ....

2 marks

Grammagators make sure they use Standard English in their schoolwork. Can you use it too?

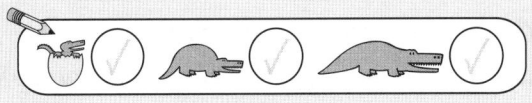

Formal and informal writing

Formal writing can sound quite serious, but informal writing is chattier and friendlier. When you're writing something important, you'll need to use formal writing.

1) Underline the parts of these sentences which make them questions, and then rewrite each sentence in formal English.

   Speech can be formal or informal too — just like writing.

   They do like chocolate cake, don't they?

   ....

   Julia will be angry if she misses the start of the race, won't she?

   ....

   All this snow will slow them down, don't you think?

   ....

   2 marks

2) Tick the version of each sentence which is written in formal English.

These geese are driving me crazy! ☐	I find these geese extremely annoying. ☐
It is very hot in here. ☐	It's boiling in here! ☐
You enjoyed feeding the kangaroos, didn't you? ☐	Did you enjoy feeding the kangaroos? ☐

   2 marks

3) Complete the sentences below with a verb in the subjunctive form.

   If I .... you, I would drop that penguin.

   It is essential that he .... the question.

   I wish I .... able to ride a unicycle.

   The subjunctive is usually only used in very formal writing and speech. Examples of the subjunctive include "If I were rich..." and "It is vital that she attend the meeting."

   2 marks

Grammagators are always on top form when they're using formal English. How did you find this page?

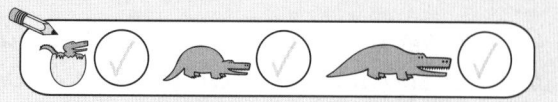

Section 5 — Writing Style

Mixed practice

Have you got the hang of writing styles? Give these questions a go, and see how you get on.

1) Underline the sentences in Non-Standard English in the passage below.

   My teacher, Mr Brigley, won an award for a production he was in last week. I seen the play, and it were really good. I've told my friends and my parents all about it. They're all gonna go see it, but I dunno when. Mr Brigley is a bit embarrassed about it all. He says he ain't used to all the attention he's bin getting. It been in all the newspapers, and he were even on TV.

   2 marks

2) Match each sentence to the correct label below.

   There's no way I'm going with her!

   We do not have any beavers.

   I would be happier if he were here.

   Gunther'll give me a call later.

   informal

   formal

   2 marks

3) Tick the sentences below that contain a verb in the subjunctive form.

   Things would be much better organised if Abby were in charge. ☐

   There was no cheese left, so we had baked beans instead. ☐

   Marian and Paula were planning to go to the library after school. ☐

   If I were a millionaire, I would buy my own zoo. ☐

   It is essential that Jeremy pay attention during the training course. ☐

   You would have enjoyed the film — it was really funny. ☐

   2 marks

Mixed practice

4) Sort these phrases into Standard English and Non-Standard English in the tables below.

- He's clever.
- That is Paulo's.
- Can you help me?
- They is silly.
- She's Charlie's daughter.
- I ain't too busy.
- We don't know nothing.
- Raj is proper pleased.
- Billy has gave it to me.
- Let's wait and see.

Standard English

He's clever ← This phrase is informal, but it follows standard grammar rules.

....

....

....

....

Non-Standard English

....

....

....

....

....

2 marks

5) Rewrite the sentences below in formal English.

They'll be sad about the ducks, don't you think?

....

We ain't got enough biscuits for all them children.

....

Lizzie didn't fancy coming camping with us.

....

2 marks

Grammagators do everything with a bit of style. How did you get on with these questions on writing style?

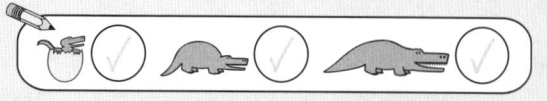

Section 6 — Making and Choosing Words

Word families

Words in a word family are all related to each other.

1) Write down which word each of these words are formed from.
   The first one has been done for you.

   helper, helpful, helped: ......help......   **calling, caller, recall:** ....

   unclear, clearly, cleared: ....   **hatred, hateful, hated:** ....

   preview, viewing, viewed: ....   **railing, derail, railway:** ....

   2 marks

2) Cross out the words that do not belong to the word families below.
   The first one has been done for you.

   sick, sickness, ~~ill~~, sickly   **swing, played, replay, playful**

   direction, route, redirect, directly   **worthwhile, worth, value, unworthy**

   2 marks

3) Draw lines to link each word family together.
   Only use each box once. The first one has been done for you.

   master — masterful
   unfamiliar — familiarity
   repeat — repetition
   repetitive
   mastery
   familiar

   2 marks

4) Look at the word family below. What does the root '**port**' mean? Tick one box.

   transport, portable, export

   have ☐   carry ☐   throw ☐   sell ☐

   1 mark

Grammagators are just one big happy family, so it's not surprising they love word families. Do you love them?

Prefixes

Prefixes are letters that are added to the beginning of words. When you add a prefix to a word, you make a new word with a different meaning.

1) Split the words below into prefixes and root words.

   disallow ⇨ .... + ...

   impatient ⇨ .... + ...

   unclear ⇨ .... + ...

   devalue ⇨ .... + ...

   2 marks

2) Underline the error in each sentence, and write the correction on the line.

   The field was undergrown with weeds. ....

   The caterpillar will semiform into a beautiful butterfly. ....

   The shipwreck was supermerged beneath the sea. ....

   Barnaby was underjoyed to see Lucinda again. ....

   2 marks

3) Use prefixes to turn the words below into two new words with opposite meanings.

   root word   **new words**

   achieve ⇨ .... and ....

   appear ⇨ .... and ....

   activate ⇨ .... and ....

   2 marks

Section 6 — Making and Choosing Words © CGP — not to be photocopied

Prefixes

4) Make as many words as you can from the prefixes and words in the table below.

Prefixes				Words			
trans	un	inter	re	do	action	lock	national

....

....

....

2 marks

5) Complete the words below by adding a prefix so that the word has the opposite meaning.

It may sound ....probable, but a meteorite has landed in our garden!

The chef's snail stew looked thoroughly ....appealing.

The house was in a state of ....repair, with broken windows and no doors.

My zip is well and truly stuck — I can't ....do it!

If I manage to ....lock the front door, I may be able to get inside.

2 marks

6) The words in these sentences have the wrong prefix.
Rewrite these sentences so that all of the words have the correct prefix.

You are misorganised and unresponsive.

....

I misagree — unfrosting a chicken takes a while!

....

2 marks

Grammagators are great at snapping prefixes onto root words. How did you get on with them?

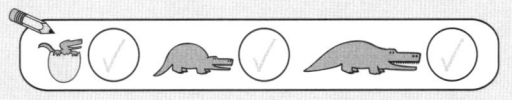

Suffixes

Suffixes are the letters you add to the end of words. Sometimes you have to change the spelling of the word when you add a suffix and sometimes you don't.

1) Write out the suffix of each of these words.

   poisonous ⇒ .... **lively** ⇒ ....

   careless ⇒ .... **cheerful** ⇒ ....

   2 marks

2) Draw lines to match the correct suffix to the following words.

   (ous)   (er)   (less)   (ate)   (ly)

   | perform | danger | fabric | faith | stupid |

   2 marks

3) Complete the sentences below by adding '**ate**', '**ise**' or '**ify**' to each word to make a verb.

   She wanted to advert............ the house in the magazine.

   I had to valid............ the ticket to claim my prize frog.

   Sadly, we didn't qual............ for the elite skipping squad.

   2 marks

4) Add a suffix to each of these nouns to make an adjective, and then use the new word in a sentence.

   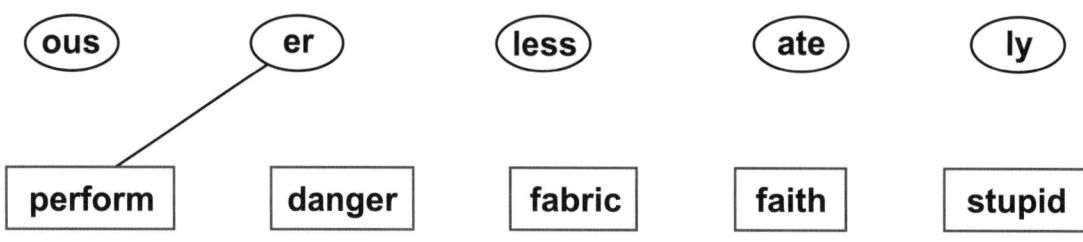

   Don't forget — the spelling of the noun may need to change before you add the suffix.

   meaning + **less** ⇒ *meaningless*

   The results of the science test are meaningless.

   practice + **al** ⇒ ....

   ....

   beauty + **ful** ⇒ ....

   ....

   2 marks

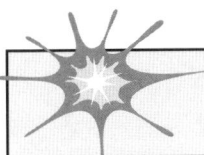

Suffixes

5) Cross out the incorrect word in the sentences below.

Rajesh felt so much (**oldest / older**) than everyone else.

I was really (**struggled / struggling**) to get all my work done.

The situation was (**hopeful / hopeless**) — we didn't stand a chance.

She felt so much (**happiness / happily**) for the new parents.

2 marks

6) Complete these sentences by adding a suffix to the word in brackets.

Heather wanted to be .... *famous* .... (fame) when she grew up.

They found it hard to .... (motive) themselves after their loss.

There were .... (few) boys than girls in the class.

Everyone received exactly the same .... (treat).

He had to .... (apology) to Olga when he lost her cat.

Water will .... (solid) if you put it in the freezer.

2 marks

7) Complete the sentences below by adding a suffix from the box to each word to make a noun.

| ness | er | ion |

The personal train.............. told Vincent to do twenty sit-ups.

Margaret was overwhelmed by Jonathan's kind.............. .

Colin's confess.............. surprised his friends.

2 marks

*Grammagators slurp down suffixes in one big gulp.
How did you get on? Tick one of the boxes.*

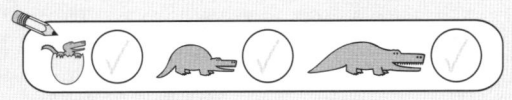

Making verbs

Making verbs — not as messy as making pancakes, but sadly not as tasty either. Have a go.

1) Complete each verb by drawing a line to the correct suffix.

he walk_		she reach_
Sandra help_	es	Rahul look_
the vase smash_	s	it touch_
it fail_		he grasp_

*he walk_* is connected to *s*. *the vase smash_* is connected to *s*.

2 marks

2) Add the suffix **-ing** to each of these verbs.

☞ *You need to double the last consonant of 'clap' before adding 'ing'.*

clap + ing ⇒ clapping   study + ing ⇒ ....

hurt + ing ⇒ ....   live + ing ⇒ ....

put + ing ⇒ ....   step + ing ⇒ ....

tie + ing ⇒ ....   train + ing ⇒ ....

2 marks

3) Add the suffix **-ed** to each of the verbs in the box to put them in the past tense. Then use each new word to complete the sentences below.

| carry ⇒ .... | cook ⇒ .... |
| chop ⇒ .... | hope ⇒ .... |

Nigel .... the vegetables with his new knife.

Lara .... she would pass her exam.

Jamie and Hugh .... the turkey to the table.

Ruby .... the pudding on her own.

2 marks

Section 6 — Making and Choosing Words   © *CGP — not to be photocopied*

Making verbs

4) Cross out the verb in each sentence that is spelt incorrectly.

The committee (**planed / planned**) to rebuild the village hall.

Anya (**moved / moveed**) to Edinburgh last month.

Mark and Dan (**packed / packked**) their suitcases very carefully.

The barber (**trimed / trimmed**) my brother's hair yesterday.

The team really (**wantted / wanted**) to win the league last season.

2 marks

5) Complete each sentence by adding **-ed** or **-ing** to the word in brackets.

Josh ....*climbed*........ (climb) the highest mountain in South America.

The waiter .... (fill) my cup to the brim.

Fiona is .... (give) Brian some vegetables.

My sisters are .... (try) to bake some scones.

We .... (beg) Niall to play basketball with us.

The llama is .... (make) a mess in your garden.

2 marks

6) Write a sentence on each of the lines using the verb and suffix given.

lie + ing ⇒ ....

jog + ed ⇒ ....

apply + ed ⇒ ....

smile + ing ⇒ ....

2 marks

Grammagators love making verbs by adding on 'ing', 'ed' and 's'. How about you — are you a Grammagator?

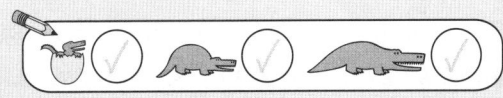

Synonyms

A synonym is a word that has the same, or nearly the same, meaning as another word.

1) Circle the word in each sentence that is a synonym for the underlined word.

   My bedroom is a <u>mess</u> — it's complete (**splendour / chaos / ruin**).

   The horse <u>nibbled</u> Mum's ear — he actually (**kissed / licked / bit**) it.

   Alim <u>carefully</u> opened the door — he (**slowly / cautiously / bravely**) pushed it.

   2 marks

2) Circle the two words in each sentence that are synonyms of each other.

   Rachel is the most fashionable person I know — her clothes are really trendy.

   I was frightened by the big brown bear because it was so extraordinarily large.

   2 marks

3) Rewrite the sentences below, replacing the underlined word with a synonym.

   A <u>strange</u> noise is coming from the kitchen.

   ....

   Judy's house was <u>completely</u> bare.

   ....

   2 marks

4) Write down as many synonyms as you can think of for the words below.

   happy ....

   quickly ....

   friend ....

   repair ....

   2 marks

Grammagators use synonyms to make their writing more interesting and less repetitive. What about you?

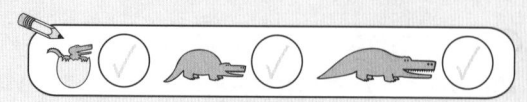

Section 6 — Making and Choosing Words

Antonyms

An antonym is a word that means the opposite of another word.

1) Draw lines to join the antonyms below. The first one has been done for you.

   fearful   confident

   unsure   boisterous

   gentle   indifferent

   despise   brave

   conscientious   adore

   2 marks

2) Complete each sentence by adding an antonym for the underlined word.

   I don't want a <u>large</u> piece — I want a .... piece.

   Don't be <u>nasty</u> to your sister — be .... to her.

   We're not allowed to talk <u>loudly</u> in here — we have to talk ....

   2 marks

3) Write an antonym for each word on the line next to it.
   Then use the antonym in a sentence.

   expensive   ....

   ....

   capture   ....

   ....

   happily   ....

   ....

   2 marks

Grammagators love antonyms — they say opposites attract. Do you like them too? Tick a box on the right.

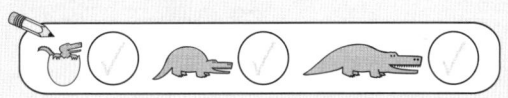

Mixed practice

Right then, the end of the book is in sight, but first you've got some mixed practice questions to deal with. Use all you've learnt in Section 6 to power through to the end.

1) Label the parts of the words that are underlined.

   Write either **prefix** or **suffix** on the lines.

   The impress<u>ive</u> dancers put on a perform<u>ance</u>.

   ....

   Sam realis<u>ed</u> that travelling by donkey is very <u>un</u>comfortable.

   ....

   2 marks

2) Draw lines to match each word to the box that contains a word from the same family.

   You can find the root word 'inform' in 'mis<u>inform</u>ed'.

   misinformed ——— inform   heater

   heating   information

   reheated   heat   informative

   2 marks

3) In each sentence, circle every prefix, and underline every suffix.

   Tomasz believ<u>ed</u> it was time to (re)join the cricket team.

   Alison was learning to ride a bicycle.

   Swimming is more fun if you completely submerge your body.

   2 marks

4) Use the suffixes in the box to complete each of the words below.

ness	ish	ible	ment	ful	ance

   employ........................   divis........................

   hurt...........................   fool.........................

   You should use each suffix once.

   empti..........................   accept......................

   2 marks

Mixed practice

5) Cross out the verbs that don't make sense in these sentences.

Steve had been (~~betraying~~ / betrayed) by his chatty parrot.

Josie was (sliced / slicing) the carrots when the doorbell rang.

Patrick (slapped / slapping) a big new sticker on the parcel.

Tanya (jumping / jumped) into the icy blue water.

The judge thought that Mr Tibbs was (deceiving / deceived) the jury.

2 marks

6) Write a synonym on the dotted line for each of the words below.

cut ⇒ ....   clever ⇒ ....

hungry ⇒ ....   bravely ⇒ ....

heal ⇒ ....   eager ⇒ ....

2 marks

7) There are six pairs of antonyms in the box below. Find them, and write the pairs on the dotted lines below. The first one has been done for you.

~~on~~	boring	dark	bottom	hard	interesting
sell	top	buy	easy	~~off~~	light

on / off ← 'on' and 'off' have opposite meanings

....

....

....

2 marks

Grammagators munch through mixed practice questions with no trouble. How have these pages been for you?

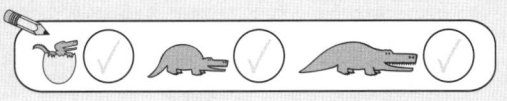

Glossary

Active — Sentences where the subject of the sentence does the action of the verb.

Adjective — A word that describes a noun, e.g. **big** house, **cold** morning.

Adverb — A word that describes a verb, an adjective or other adverbs.

Adverbial — A word, or group of words, that behaves like an adverb. It gives more information about a verb or clause.

Antonyms — Words that mean the opposite, e.g. **big** and **small**.

Clause — Part of a sentence that contains a subject and a verb.

Conjunction — A word that joins two clauses or sentences, e.g. **and**, **but**, **so**.

Determiner — A word that tells you if a noun is general or specific, e.g. **the**, **a** or **an**.

Main clause — A clause that makes sense on its own,
e.g. <u>I went out</u> even though it was raining.
This bit is the main clause because 'I went out' makes sense on its own.

Modal verb — A verb that can show how likely something is, e.g. **We <u>might</u> go out.**

Noun — A word that names something, e.g. **Paul**, **scissors**, **herd**, **happiness**.

Object — The part of the sentence that the action of the verb is being done to.

Passive — Sentences where the subject has something done to it.

Glossary

Phrase — A small part of a sentence, usually without a verb.

Possessive pronoun — A pronoun which shows who owns something, e.g. **mine**, **hers**.

Prefix — Letters that can be put in front of a word to change its meaning, e.g. **un**lock.

Preposition — A word that tells you how things are related, e.g. **in**, **above**, **before**.

Pronoun — Words that can be used instead of nouns, e.g. **I**, **you**, **he**, **it**.

Relative clause — A type of subordinate clause that tells you more about a noun. It is often introduced by a relative pronoun, e.g. **She's the girl who likes onions.**

Relative pronoun — A pronoun that introduces a relative clause, e.g. **who**, **which**, **that**.

Subject — The person or thing doing the action of the verb.

Subordinate clause — A clause which doesn't make sense on its own, e.g. **While you were out, I watched TV.**

This bit is the subordinate clause because 'While you were out' doesn't make sense on its own.

Suffix — Letters that can be put after a word to change its meaning, e.g. play**ful**.

Synonyms — Words that mean the same, e.g. **large** and **big**.

Verb — A doing or being word, e.g. I **run**, he **went**, you **are**.

Scoresheet

Fill in your scores below, then add them up to find your total marks.

Section 1	Score
Nouns	/ 6
Singular and plural nouns	/ 8
Types of noun	/ 14
Pronouns	/ 12
Determiners	/ 6
Verbs	/ 23
Adjectives	/ 12
Adverbs	/ 12
Mixed practice	/ 28
Total for Section 1	**/ 121**
Section 2	**Score**
Sentences	/ 6
Paragraphs	/ 5
Phrases	/ 12
Clauses	/ 12
Relative clauses	/ 11
Mixed practice	/ 26
Total for Section 2	**/ 72**
Section 3	**Score**
Co-ordinating conjunctions	/ 5
Subordinating conjunctions	/ 5
Prepositions	/ 14
Mixed practice	/ 15
Total for Section 3	**/ 39**

Section 4	Score
Subject and object	/ 6
Active and passive voice	/ 6
Past, present and future tenses	/ 13
Verbs with 'have'	/ 6
Verbs with '-ing'	/ 6
Mixed practice	/ 14
Total for Section 4	**/ 51**
Section 5	**Score**
Standard vs. Non-Standard	/ 14
Formal and informal writing	/ 6
Mixed practice	/ 10
Total for Section 5	**/ 30**
Section 6	**Score**
Word families	/ 7
Prefixes	/ 12
Suffixes	/ 14
Making verbs	/ 12
Synonyms	/ 8
Antonyms	/ 6
Mixed practice	/ 14
Total for Section 6	**/ 73**
Total for Book	**386**

Look at your total score to see how you're doing and where you need more practice:

0 – 230 — You've made a good start. Revise grammar and then have another go.

231 – 330 — You're doing well. Have another look at any sections you're struggling with.

331 – 386 — You're doing really well. Give yourself a pat on the back.